THE LITTLE BOOK OF TRAVEL

Basic Phrases for travel
Imagine situations as they may happen.
Listen for your Cue word.
Keep English simple

By
Robin J. Okano

Imagine situations as they may happen. Listen for CUE words.
What should you say? Focus on KEYWORDS.
Keep English simple.

INTRODUCTION
NEED TO KNOW WORDS

QUESTION KEYS   DON'T BE SHY
ALWAYS POLITE   WORDS FOR ALL OCCASIONS

QUESTION KEYS   HOW TO ASK

"W" question words

WHAT
Explains

What is it?
What is the exchange rate?
What happened?

WHAT TIME
Time

What time is it?
What is the local time?
What time does it start?

WHEN
Time

When is dinner?
When do we leave?
When is the vacation?

WHERE
Direction / Place

Where can I sit?
Where is the restroom?
Where is the station?

WHO/WHOM
Person

Who are you?
Whom should I ask?
Who would know?

WHICH
Choice

Which is mine?
Which do you want?
Which way do we go?

WHY
Explains

Why is that?
Why do you want to go?
Why did they leave?

i

QUESTION KEYS	HOW TO ASK
"H" question words	
HOW	How are you?
Explains	How do I use this?
	How does it work?
HOW MUCH	How much is it?
Price/Amount	How much time do we have?
	How much work is there?
HOW MANY	How many?
Amount	How many are there?
	How many do I need?
HOW LONG	How long is it?
Distance/time	How long will it take?
	How long is this bridge?
HOW FAR	How far is it?
Distance	How far is the station?
	How far are we going?

What kind of question do you want to ask?
Keywords: plus "W" question or "H" question
Keep it simple
   1. What time do we arrive?   Time/arrive = Keywords +What
   2. How much is this bag?   Much/bag = Keywords + How

HOW TO ANSWER   LISTEN FOR KEYWORDS **"W"** or **"H"**
   1. Use the same words in reverse.
   2. Repeat the question to yourself or say it out loud:
     What time do *we arrive*?   Answer: Reverse   *We arrive* at 10:00.
     How *much* is the *bag*?   Answer: Reverse   *The bag* is $100.00.

ALWAYS POLITE

In English politeness is expressed by the inflection in our voice and the stance of our posture. There are some "polite" words, but remember, everything can be said politely with a friendly tone of voice, a pleasant attitude and a SMILE. The order: "Go over there", becomes a request when you add "Please". *Please, go over there.* (Put a smile in your voice and on your face.)

ALWAYS POLITE
MAY   PLEASE   THANK YOU   YOU'RE WELCOME   EXCUSE ME
1. May I? = May I help you?
2. May I please? = May I take one?
3. Yes, you may. Or I'm sorry. No, you may not.
4. Thank you very much.
5. Yes, thank you. = Answers a question + Thank you. Ex: Would you like some more chicken?
6. No, thank you. = Answers a question + Thank you. No + Thank you + smile is very polite.
7. You're welcome: *My pleasure* or more casually, *No problem, No worries* or *That's okay.*
8. Excuse me: Asking for assistance Or *Excuse me, can you help me, please?*
9. Excuse me: *I'm sorry* or *I beg your pardon.*

When asking a question
Simple, direct questions
   1. Would you like to go to the movies?
      Answer: Yes, I would. Thank you.
Someone may ask you a polite but confusing question in the negative.... How do you answer? Negative polite questions using
DON'T   CAN'T   WOULDN'T   ISN'T
   1. Don't you want something to drink?   Would you like something to drink?
      Answer: Yes, please, thank you.   Or   No, thank you. (I don't want anything.)
   2. Can't I get you something to eat?   May I get you something to eat?
      Answer: Yes, please, thank you.   Or   No, thank you I'm okay.
   3. Wouldn't you like to buy this?   Would you like to buy this?
      Answer: Yes, I would like to buy it.   Or   No, thank you.
   4. Isn't the theater here?   Is the theater here?
      Answer: Yes, it is here.   Or   No, it's not here.

DON'T BE SHY

Try to speak in a loud, clear voice with eye-contact. Don't mumble. Say what you mean but of course politely with a kind tone of voice, put a smile in your voice. When you don't understand something, don't be timid ask a question. If you did not hear something request it to be repeated. Using the word PLEASE is polite and shows your respect.

PHRASES TO MEMORIZE AND SAY QUICKLY AND EASILY
1. Excuse me.......
2. Pardon me
3. That's all right.
4. My name is.......
5. May I have your name please?
6. I didn't catch your name.
7. I don't understand.
8. Please explain
9. Please speak slower.
10. Do you mind repeating that, please?
11. Would you repeat that, please?
12. How do you spell that, please
13. Please, write it here.
14. What does this mean?
15. I can't hear you.
16. Please hurry.
17. I want....... please.
18. I'm looking for....... Thank you.
19. I haven't decided.
20. Thank you but no thank you.

WORDS FOR ALL OCCASIONS

Learn to fill the gaps of conversations with pleasant, polite and easy to say expressions.
Conversation has a rhythm of two people speaking together, 1-2-1-2. It is not a 1-1-1-1-1-1-1 then a 2-2-2-2-2-2-2 type of rhythm. Of course while you listen it is important to express understanding, amazement, doubt or shock with words and a nod or shaking of the head.

WORDS FOR ALL OCCASIONS   To keep the 1-2-1-2-1-2 rhythm

1. Is that right?   Agreement
2. Yes, yes, yes.   Agreement
3. I see   Understanding
4. Absolutely   Agreement
5. Really?   Amazement
6. You're kidding?   Doubt
7. Oh, no!   Shock

GREETINGS   SALUTATIONS   LEAVE-TAKING   ADIEU

Expressing good wishes gives you confidence and also builds friendships.

1. Good morning.... Good afternoon.... Good evening.... Good night
2. How do you do?
3. Nice to meet you.
4. It's a pleasure to meet you.
5. Good-bye. Nice to have met you.
6. Hope to see you again, soon.
7. How are you?
8. Fine, thank you and you?
9. How's it going?
10. Everything's great, and you?
11. How are things?
12. Things are so-so, and you?
13. How have you been?
14. Nice weather, isn't it?
15. It's a little chilly, isn't it?
16. It's getting warmer, don't you think?
17. Give my regards to your family.
18. Take care of yourself.
19. Thanks for your help.
20. See you soon.

TABLE OF CONTENTS

Page

Introduction Need to know words ··· i
Question Keys ·· ii
Always polite ··· iii
Don't be shy ·· iv
Words for all occasions ··· v

1. IN THE PLANE ·· 1
   International flight
2. AT THE AIRPORT ··· 7
   Getting through Immigrations and Customs
3. GETTING TO THE HOTEL ·· 13
   Rent-a-car, bus, taxi-cab or train
4. AT THE HOTEL / CONDOMINIUM ························· 19
   Checking in and finding the amenities
5. AT THE RESTAURANT ··· 25
   Ordering your first meal
6. GOING SHOPPING ·· 31
   Finding the best buy
7. GOING SIGHTSEEING ·· 37
   Traveling by bus, train or plane domestically
8. MEETING A FAMILY ··· 43
   Visiting a family or a homestay experience
9. AT THE THEATER ··· 49
   Encountering culture and entertainment
10. AT THE SUPERMARKET/DRUGSTORE ················ 55
    Getting the things you need by yourself

Notes ·· 61

1. IN THE PLANE
INTERNATIONAL FLIGHT

SITUATION

Whether you have a paper tour ticket or E-ticket you form a line at the airline's counter. Here your luggage (at airports it is called baggage) is weighed and you receive baggage stubs with numbers. These numbers will assist the airlines if unfortunately they misplace your bag. Your ticket is exchanged for a boarding-pass with your seat number and gate information, where and when the plane will depart. Now, you check the time; say good-bye to the friends who have come to see you off on your adventure and turn and walk alone through to customs and immigrations. Your hand luggage (carry-on bag) is X-rayed and you proceed to immigrations, where your passport is stamped verifying that you have left Japan. On the way to your gate you will pass by souvenir shops that offer last chance to buy Japanese snacks and Duty-Free shops. At your departure gate, when your seat group is called once again you show your passport and boarding pass. As you enter the plane a stewardess checks your boarding pass and tells you which side of the plane your seat is on, right or left, aisle, middle or window. You find your seat; put your carry-on in the overhead compartment and any bag you may want during the flight under the seat in front of you. You sit back and fasten your seatbelt and prepare for take-off. Once in the air the stewardesses have a scheduled routine to make your flight a pleasant one.

WHAT HAPPENS NEXT

1. You watch the video of safety features and emergency directions. Pay attention.
2. Your seat pocket has earphones, waterproof air-sickness bags and magazines.
3. The Airline magazine has directions for completing Immigrations & Customs forms.
4. Hot towels are passed out with the Menu for Food and Beverages.
5. You are offered something to drink; anything with alcohol might cost money.
6. You are served dinner or a light meal depending on the time.
7. While flying over international waters you have an opportunity to buy duty-free items.
8. You sit back and enjoy the audio / video programs that have been arranged.
9. Before arrival you are served another meal with beverages, all on the Menu.
10. You have completed and signed your foreign Immigrations and Customs forms.

NEED TO KNOW VOCABULARY

1. Emergency Exit
2. Fasten Seatbelts
3. Oxygen mask
4. Life-vest
5. Turbulence
6. International Dateline
7. Jet lag
8. Tray table
9. Toilet / lavatory....... Vacant / Occupied
10. Return seats to their upright position
11. Aisle seat
12. Window seat

1. IN THE PLANE

QUESTIONS AND ANSWERS FOR PAIR TALKING

1. What are the initials of your Airport destination?
    I'll have to check the code listings.
    I know SFO and NRT.
    I need this for E-tickets.
2. How many people are traveling with you and how many bags are you checking?
    I'm by myself with 2 bags.
    There are two of us with 2 bags each.
    I'm with a tour
3. Do you have a Japanese language newspaper?
    Yes, we have Asahi, Nihon Keizai, and Sankei.
    No, sorry we only have English newspapers.
4. Excuse me what is the local time? I want to change my watch.
    Good idea, it is 3AM.
    Oh of course, it is 3PM.
    Let me check for you.
5. Can you be responsible for the emergency door?
    No, may I change seats, please?
    Yes, what do I need to do?
    Will you help me?
6. How do I turn on the overhead light?
    It's on the remote control.
    Be careful of Stewardess call-button.
    It's on the side panel.
7. Where is my life-vest?
    It's under your seat.
    The seat cushion is the life-vest.
    It is in the arm rest.
8. Where is the oxygen mask?
    It automatically drops down from the overhead bin.
    Put yours on first then help others.

9. Where is my tray table?
   It flips down from this seat-back.
   It is in the arm rest.
   Sorry, we need to bring it to you.
10. Can we avoid turbulence?
    I hope so, but always keep your seatbelt fastened.
    If you sleep, please fasten your seatbelt.

PHRASES TO RECOGNIZE AND REMEMBER

1. Please return your seat to its upright position.
2. There is a little turbulence please return to your seats and fasten your seatbelts.
3. This is a non-smoking flight.
4. If you are in transit please follow the signs for the transit lounge.
5. If you are transferring flights first go through customs then an airline official will assist you.
6. We hope you had a pleasant flight and look forward to serving you again. Thank You

CONVERSATIONS

Memorize the sentences then try to write your own conversation

Conversation 1
Listen for the Keywords

A: I'm really nervous about speaking and hearing English on this trip.
B: Listen for the keyword.... that's your cue to speak. It's simple.
A: Now I really am nervous.
B: There are lots of ways to say the same thing, so listen and think what is being said.
A: Like, "Would you like something to drink?" or "Do you want something to drink?"

1. IN THE PLANE

B: Exactly. The keyword is drink.... the stewardess might even say, "Do you care for a drink?"

Conversation 2
Listen with your eyes
A: Even if I understand the keyword how do I answer politely?
B: Simple, just say "Please, Thank you or No, Thank you." Think words not sentences.
A: Like, "Chicken, please."
B: See it's easy....use your eyes to listen...pay attention to what is happening and smile.
A: Ok. Now I'm cold and sleepy... so I'll say, "Blanket... pillow... please." with a smile.
B: You got it... You can say, "May I have a blanket and pillow, please?" Be confident, smile.

Conversation 3
Write your *Plane* conversation using vocabulary words
A:
B:
A:
B:
A:
B:

FILL IN THE BLANKS

From the list below select the correct word or words to complete each sentence.

aisle   pay   occupied   oxygen mask   window   air-sickness bag   menu seatbelt   turbulence   video   immigrations   customs   vacant   life-vest

1. When you watch the _____ on safety instructions it is important to _____ attention.
2. Your seat packet contains an _____ as well as earphones.
3. You must complete the _____ and _____ forms before disembarking, deplaning.
4. An _____ seat allows you to have more leg room.
5. A _____ seat has a view.
6. The _____ explains what food will be served during the flight.
7. For safety in flight always keep your _____ fastened.
8. If there is a storm you might experience some _____.
9. Your _____ is under your seat and the _____ will drop down from the overhead bin.
10. When someone is in the lavatory it means that it is _____ and the sign will say that.

ESSAY

Write your *Airplane story*.... even if you have never traveled by plane imagine what it might be like. Use the words and sentences in this chapter.

2. AT THE AIRPORT...GETTING THROUGH IMMIGRATIONS AND CUSTOMS

SITUATION

You have arrived at your destination. As you leave the plane you follow the signs for Immigrations and Baggage Claim. The Stewardess has announced on which rack your bags will be, according to the flight number...i.e. JAL 001 Rack B. Now you simply follow the signs to Immigrations. Here you will be expected to present your passport and the immigration form you completed in the plane. Each person traveling with his own passport must complete this form. Be sure that you have signed it, your signature in cursive letters, not block. You will be asked several questions about your trip and accommodations. You might be fingerprinted/ hand printed, have a snap shot taken or even eye identification recorded. After the immigration official stamps your passport you enter the baggage area and retrieve your bag from the proper rack. With bags in hand you proceed to Customs. Here you present the other form that you filled out on the plane, one per family and also signed. Again you may be asked questions and your bags may be opened or X-rayed. If you are continuing on another flight look for information about baggage check-in. If this is your final destination you might want to look for a bank to exchange your money and then for transportation to your hotel. Welcome to your adventure in this New Country! Have Fun! Pay Attention.

WHAT HAPPENS NEXT

1. In the plane you have completed the Immigrations and Customs forms.
2. You disembark and follow the signs to Immigrations and Baggage Claim.
3. An Immigration officer will ask you questions about your journey.
4. You will be finger printed maybe even have eye identification.
5. You proceed to the baggage area and find your flight's baggage rack. i.e. B JAL 001
6. Go to Customs.... give the Customs Officer your completed customs form.
7. You may be asked to open your bags or explain any gifts you have.
8. Once passed Customs if you need cash look for a Money Exchange booth.
9. Now you walk out the outward swinging doors or gate into this new country.
10. Look for transportation to your hotel, shuttle bus or rent-a-car.

NEED TO KNOW VOCABULARY

Immigrations
1. Disembarkation Card
2. Embarkation Card (Lower part of card must be turned in when leave country)
3. Last name/Family name
4. First name/Given name
5. Nationality... Passport... Issuing Authority
6. Date of Birth (USA: Month, Day and Year UK: Day, Month and Year)
7. Permanent Address
8. Country of Residence
9. Occupation
10. Purpose of trip... Sightseeing.... Business.... Other
11. Address: Where staying in Country
12. Final Destination
13. Quarantine

2. AT THE AIRPORT

QUESTIONS AND ANSWERS FOR PAIR TALKING

Questions from an immigration officer
1. Is this your first visit here?
    Yes, I'm looking forward to it.
    No, this is my second visit.
2. What is the purpose of your trip?
    I'm visiting for sightseeing.
    I'm here on business.
    I'm here to study.
3. Where are you staying?
    I'm staying at this address.
    I'm staying at this hotel.
    I'm staying at the school dormitory.
4. How long do you intend/plan/to stay?
    I'll be here for 2 weeks.
    I'll be here for 2 months.
    I'm attending school for a year.

Questions at Baggage Claim and Customs
5. I can't find my bags. What should I do?
    Do you have your baggage claim number?
    Please fill out a description sheet.   How many bags?
6. How many people are traveling with you?
    I'm by myself.
    There are three of us.
    We are a family of four.
7. Where do I check-in my bags for my connecting flight?
    Put them on that rack.
    We'll take them.
    You have to carry them out.
8. Do you have anything to declare?
    No, these are only my personal effects.
    I have four bottles of wine.
    These are gifts.

9. Do you have any foods, fruit or meats?
   I have dried seaweed and rice crackers.
   I have powder tea.
   I have pickles.
10. Is there public transportation into town?
    You can get the shuttle bus on the corner.
    The taxi stand is over there.
    Your hotel has a bus.

PHRASES TO RECOGNIZE AND REMEMBER
1. What is the purpose of your trip?
2. How long are you planning to stay?
3. Do you have any fruits, fresh foods or meats?
4. Please open your bags.
5. Do you have any gifts?
6. What is the exchange rate?

CONVERSATIONS
Memorize the sentences then try to write your own conversation

Conversation 1
At Immigrations and Customs
A: Welcome. May I see your passport, and immigration paper? Is this your first trip here?
B: Yes, I'm going to be studying at a summer English program. Here are the enrollment papers.
A: Okay, these look good. Please take your finger prints, right thumb first.
B: Thank you.
C: Do you have the customs paper? Do you have anything to declare?
B: No, these are only my things.

2. AT THE AIRPORT

Conversation 2
Money Exchange
A: Can you cash this Traveler's Check, please?
B: Certainly, please sign here, oh, you need to sign here at the top first so no one can take them.
A: Thank you I forgot. Can you give me 3 $20's... 2 $10's... 3 $5's...and 4 $1's and change.
B: You can use the Traveler's Checks to purchase things at stores. If you sign first they are safe.
A: How long do the banks stay open?
B: We're open from 9-6 on weekdays and until noon on Saturday. Sunday is a holiday.

Conversation 3
Write your *Immigrations and Customs* conversation using vocabulary words
A:
B:
A:
B:
A:
B:

11

FILL IN THE BLANKS

From the list below select the correct word or words to complete each sentence.

last   passport   flight number   traveler's checks   signature   sightseeing business   exchange rate   questions   shuttle bus   transit

1. When you write your name in cursive letters this is called your _____.
2. Your family name is your _____ name.
3. When flying internationally besides a ticket and _____ you might need a visa.
4. The immigration officer will ask you _____ about your itinerary.
5. If you are on a sightseeing trip your purpose is _____.
6. When locating your bags look for the rack with the proper airlines and _____.
7. If you are continuing on to another destination you are in _____.
8. When changing to local money you want the best _____.
9. There are several ways to carry money, cash, credit cards and _____.
10. A _____ can take you to your hotel.

ESSAY

Write your *At the Airport* story use the words and sentences in the chapter.

3. GETTING TO THE HOTEL
RENT-A-CAR, BUS, TAXI-CAB or TRAIN

SITUATION:

Congratulations, now that you are through customs, you are in the main area of the airport. If you have made arrangements before traveling for a rent-a-car and have your International driver's license, look for signs for that company i.e. Avis, Budget or National. It is possible to rent a car from any of the companies at the airport even without a reservation. You must have a credit card and buy insurance. The companies provide local maps and activity information. If you are planning an extended stay it might even be cheaper to rent from a local dealer in town.

If you are not renting a car, look for the Bus stop for the local hotel shuttles. Most likely there will be a free shuttle to your hotel or a shuttle that goes to the downtown area. Be sure to ask the driver if he stops at your hotel. If you are in a hurry and are willing to pay a little more than a taxi/cab is best. You should expect to tip the driver. While at the airport take a minute to look for maps and activity brochures, although your hotel will have a concierge who can help you with your itinerary. In asking questions for directions pay attention to the answers. You might have to write them down or keep asking until you understand. Don't be shy.

WHAT HAPPENS NEXT

1. You have exited customs and are now in the arrival lobby of the airport of your new country.
2. You look for a Tourist Information Center to inquire about the best way to get to your hotel.
3. You gather maps and information of potential visiting sites and itinerary plans.
4. You've studied what you want to see and do but now you gather information in English.
5. You've reserved a rent-a-car or want to do so, now you look for the companies.
6. You have a credit card which enables you to rent a car now you must buy car insurance.
7. Your hotel has a shuttle bus to and from the airport.
8. There are shuttle buses that stop at or near your hotel. You ask the driver before you board.
9. You're eager to start your trip so you take a taxi/cab and add a tip to the fare.
10. You ask questions until you understand and even take notes on the answers.

NEED TO KNOW VOCABULARY

1. Itinerary
2. Car insurance
3. Reserved / Confirmation
4. Reservations
5. Danger
6. Keep Out / Off Limits / No Trespassing
7. Under Construction
8. Out of Order
9. Warning
10. Wet Paint

3. GETTING TO THE HOTEL

QUESTIONS AND ANSWERS FOR PAIR TALKING

1. Excuse me, where is the Tourist Information Center?
    Go straight down that aisle.
    It's in the next terminal.
    It's upstairs.
    It's downstairs.
2. Is there a bus to the center of the city?
    You'll need exact change.
    It runs every 15 minutes.
    There are several.
3. How much is a taxi? / What is the taxi fare?
    For 3 people a taxi is cheaper.
    You need to tip the driver.
    Make sure you have small change.
4. Can I rent a car at the airport?
    Of course, you need an International license.
    Of course but you need a credit card.
5. I have a reservation for a car.
    Do you want a US or Japanese make?
    Do you want GPS?
    Did you want the sedan or van?
6. Do I need to return the car with a full tank of gas?
    That's an option.
    It's better to buy gas in town.
    You can refill when you return the car.
7. May I drop the car at my destination?
    Our companies are in major cities.
    Please return it to the airport.
    We can make arrangements.
8. Is there a subway or train into town?
    There is a street car at the corner.
    The train station is over there.
    The subway stops at midnight.

15

9. Does the shuttle bus go to the hotel?
   It stops at all major hotels.
   You'll have to walk a block.
   It runs every 20 minutes.
10. How do I return to the airport?
    You can get a taxi/cab.
    Walk to the shuttle pick-up stop.
    A bus leaves from the hotel.

PHRASES TO RECOGNIZE AND REMEMBER

1. This shuttle goes to all major hotels.
2. Press the buzzer when you want to get off.
3. Please exit from the back/front/middle of the bus.
4. Registration for sightseeing tours is available from your hotel.
5. Do you have your confirmation papers for the car you reserved?
6. What type of insurance will you need?

CONVERSATIONS

Memorize the sentences then try to write your own conversation

Conversation 1
Rent-a-car

A: Are you sure you want to drive on your trip.
B: Yes, I very excited. I've studied all the roads and signs and memorized the names.
A: You know you need an International driver's license, a credit card and car insurance.
B: No problem. I am worried about speed and driving on the opposite side of the road.
A: Speed is addictive be careful, by the way just remember to pass drivers shoulder to shoulder.

3. GETTING TO THE HOTEL

B: Oh, when an oncoming car nears, we drivers are opposite each other, shoulder to shoulder.

Conversation 2
Getting there by bus
A: I'm nervous about taking public transportation.
B: The airport "Information Center" can help you... just tell them where you want to go.
A: How do you travel? I heard some places you have to open the door yourself to exit.
B: It's best to study about available transportation and systems before you go.
A: Yes, I can understand that and also the looks of the currency...no surprises with money.
B: Find out if a One-day travel card or Long-tern travel pass for trains and subways is available.

Conversation 3
Write your *Transportation* conversation using vocabulary words
A:
B:
A:
B:
A:
B:

17

FILL IN THE BLANKS

From the list below select the correct word or words to complete the sentence.

concierge exit reservation attention license confirmation maps information center insurance check-in shuttle wet paint

1. When asking directions you pay _____ and even take notes.
2. The hotel's _____ can help you with any problems.
3. To rent a car you need a credit card and an International driver's _____.
4. To drive the car you need to buy car _____ too.
5. You memorized all the local street names and landmarks and you've brought _____.
6. You have your hotel _____ but it is still too early to _____.
7. When you do register, you give the hotel front your _____ voucher.
8. The bus driver asks you to _____ from the center of the bus.
9. An _____ is located in the center of the airport and also downtown.
10. As you sit on the park bench you wonder what the _____ sign means.

ESSAY

Write your *Getting to the hotel* story. Use the words and sentences in the chapter.

4. AT THE HOTEL / CONDOMINIUM
CHECKING IN AND FINDING THE AMENITIES

SITUATION

You have arrived at your hotel and go to the "front" or check-in counter. Perhaps you have a confirmation voucher but you will still need to fill out an address form. The person "checking you in" will explain the procedure and tell you about some of the activities, programs and amenities in and around your location. If you are staying in a hotel the Front Desk will ask a Bell Hop to show you to your room and help you with your bags. Once at the room you must tip the Bell Hop for helping you. (Ask the appropriate amount to tip, for example $1.50 per bag.)

If you are in a condominium, you'll receive your key and verbal directions to your room. There may also be a complimentary breakfast included in your stay. For example, the first morning during breakfast the condominium's travel consultant might give a small presentation of all the activities available to you during your stay. There may also be free tickets or discounts to special events.

In a hotel the usual accommodations are a room with a bath. In a condominium your accommodation are more like a small apartment equipped with a kitchen, with cooking and eating utensils. It is possible to buy groceries and make your own meals. This is a pleasant convenience for a group of friends or families with small children. In a hotel you will have room service but in a condominium you can do things for yourself. There is usually a washer-dryer facility available for a nominal fee, plus you supply the soap. Room cleaning is the same in both types, everyday with a change of towels. It is polite to leave this maid service $1.00 for each bed. This must be placed on the pillow, not the side table. Which to choose is up to your situation and demands. A hotel offers luxury and service. A condominium allows for freedom to "do it yourself". It is a home away from home for your group or family plus it is a little more casual.

WHAT HAPPENS NEXT

1. You show the front desk your reservation and confirmation voucher.
2. You fill in the registration forms, including name and address in home country.
3. If you have a rent-a-car you request a parking permit. There might be an extra fee.
4. The hotel person tells you about activities.
5. A Bell Hop helps you with your bags but expects a tip. Or you say, "Thank you, I can manage."
6. A complementary first breakfast may be included plus an orientation spiel.
7. You are self-reliant in a condominium and cook and wash for yourself.
8. You leave $1.00 on each pillow for room cleaning and a change of towels and linen.
9. You look for the Laundromat on your floor of the condominium to do your wash.
10. You relax in the luxury of a hotel or enjoy the casual "at home" ambiance of a condominium together with a group of friends or your family.

NEED TO KNOW VOCABULARY

1. Package deals
2. Voucher
3. Time Shares
4. Bed and Breakfast
5. Oven
6. Do not disturb / Please make up the room

4. AT THE HOTEL / CONDOMINIUM

QUESTIONS AND ANSWERS FOR PAIR TALKING

1. I have a reservation for today, may I check in now?
   You may register but check-in is at 2:00.
   Sorry, but you may leave your bags here.
2. Does everyone need to fill out a card?
   Just the responsible person.
   Please write your contact information.
3. Do you have a roll-away bed?
   Room service will bring it.
   The sofa opens up to a double bed.
   There are blankets and sheets.
4. How do I turn on the lights?
   Your room card activates the switch.
   When you're in your room keep your card in the slot.
5. Is there a beauty salon or barber shop in the hotel?
   Yes, on the 2nd floor.
   Yes, in the underground mall.
   There are boutiques and restaurants.
6. Where is the Laundromat?
   One is located on every odd numbered floor.
   It is in the basement. You need soap and quarters.
7. Is there a life guard on duty?
   Swim at your own risk.
   Only from 11〜2.
   Parents must be responsible for their children.
8. Is there a near-by supermarket?
   Essentials are available on the 5th floor.
   There is one on the next block.
   It's around the corner.
9. What time is check-out?
   11 AM
   12 Noon
   You can store your bags until flight time.

10. How do I get to the airport?
    Take the shuttle bus.
    Shall I call a taxi?
    The local bus goes by the airport.

PHRASES TO REMEMBER

1. I have a reservation for a single room. Here is my confirmation.
2. Is there an internet outlet in my room?
3. Please bring a rollaway bed.
4. How do I turn off/on the heater... the air conditioner?
5. Are there any shops in the hotel?
6. Where is the gym? Where is the Laundromat?
7. What are the pool hours? Is there a lifeguard on duty?
8. Can anyone use the barbeque? Is there a fee?
9. What time is check-out?
10. Is there a limousine or shuttle bus to the airport?

CONVERSATIONS

Memorize the sentences then try to write your own conversation

Conversation 1
By the room or by the person

A: A condominium is so convenient for group travel.
B: Yes, you can be casual and independent.
A: You pay for the room, so as many as six people can stay together.
B: You might have two bedrooms plus the living room sofa pulls out as an extra bed.
A: Everything is furnished even the kitchen has pans and utensils for cooking.
B: It's bigger than my apartment in Tokyo, everything is big and relaxing. It's fantastic.

4. AT THE HOTEL / CONDOMINIUM

Conversation 2
Hotel Check-in
A: There are two families in our group; do you have a connecting room?
B: Yes, the corner room on the 10th floor is connecting.
A: Great, I'd like to check-in now. Here is my passport for identification.
B: Please fill in the information on the card.
A: Do you need a local address?
B: No, just your current address in your home country.

Conversation 3
Write your *Accommodations* conversation using vocabulary words
A:
B:
A:
B:
A:
B:

FILL IN THE BLANKS

From the list below select the correct word or words to complete the sentences.

*permit free Laundromat oven amenities do-not-disturb
bed and breakfast condominium tip voucher luxury*

1. The clerk at the front desk explains the activities and _____ at the hotel.
2. What is the appropriate amount to _____ in a taxi, hotel or restaurant?
3. If you want to keep your car in the parking lot you'll need a parking _____.
4. In a _____ you can do things for yourself and it is more casual than a hotel.
5. If something is complimentary it means that it is _____.
6. I want to wash my clothes where is the _____?
7. The kitchen has a microwave, refrigerator, stove and _____.
8. It's nice to do for yourself but on a vacation I want the _____ of a hotel.
9. Besides a hotel or condominium you can also stay in a _____ or Inn.
10. If you want to sleep late just hang the _____ sign on the door.

ESSAY

Write your *Accommodations* story. Use the words and sentences in this chapter.

5. AT THE RESTAURANT
ORDERING YOUR FIRST MEAL

SITUATION

You've settled into your accommodations and now you're ready to get something to eat. All restaurants are not the same. Most family style cafes do not serve alcohol including beer. Many places with an "atmosphere" might have a dress code, i.e. neckties and jackets for men. Even at a beach resort many restaurants require customers to wear shoes as opposed to beach sandals. Regardless of the type of eating place you have selected unless it is self-service or drive-through a 15% tip is required when you leave. (Sometimes the tip is included in the bill.) If you plan on eating at the same place again it is a good idea to tip. If you liked the food and the service was good you should tip. In many establishments wages for waiters and waitresses are low; they depend on tips to make a living. Good service is always prompt, plenty of water if you've asked for it, explaining the menu and after the food is served occasionally asking, "Is everything okay?" If you come as a family parents are expected to control their children in public...children cannot run freely around the dining room.

If the waiter has made a mistake in your order, you should complain. If there is a bug in your salad you should complain. If you want your meat cooked more you should tell the waiter. If you are pleasant in your complaints and not demanding people will help you willingly. Be gracious but firm. Eating is one of the joys of life. Everyone is working to make your dining experience one to remember. Bon Appétit !

WHAT HAPPENS NEXT

1. You walk into a restaurant and ask for a table for 2.
2. You call ahead of time and make a reservation. It's a simple way to guarantee a table.
3. You say your name, Okano. Spell it to be sure, O-K-A-N-O.
4. You say the number of people in your group. "I'd like to reserve a table for 6 at 8:00."
5. You ask for the place you'd like to sit, a view, a window, a quiet area or no smoking area.
6. You ask if there is a dress code and if so, "What is it?"
7. You go to the restaurant, sign your name on the register and receive a paging beeper.
8. Your waiter speaks slowly and explains the menu. He patiently answers your questions.
9. Your waiter stops by your table to bring more water or to see if everything is okay.
10. You enjoy your meal and tip the waiter 15% of the bill.

NEED TO KNOW VOCABULARY

1. Soup of the day
2. À la cart
3. Main course
4. House Specialty
5. Sommelier
6. Chef's signature dish
7. Take out
8. Side order
9. Appetizer
10. Dessert
11. Non-Alcoholic Beverage
12. Doggy bag

5. AT THE RESTAURANT

QUESTIONS AND ANSWERS FOR PAIR TALKING

1. Would you like to make a reservation?
    Yes, a table for 2.
    Yes, a table for 5 at 6:00.
    Yes, do you have a table by a window?
2. May I have your name, please? How many will be in your party?
    Okano, there are 10 of us. O-k-a-n-o.
    Sekiguchi, we have 8 in our group.
3. Is there an evening dress code?
    Yes, jackets and ties for men.
    Please wear shoes, no beach sandals.
    No, dress is informal.
4. May I register our reservation now? How does the beeper work?
    Yes, sign here, we'll buzz you.
    Write your name here, a light will come on.
    Yes, it's easy.
5. How long is the wait?
    It won't be long now.
    It's about 20 minutes.
    You're the next group on the list.
6. Do you have a child's menu?
    Yes, it's on the back.
    I'm sorry but we can do 1/2 orders.
    Yes, we have special dishes.
7. I have an allergy, are there onions in the sauce?
    I'll check with the cook.
    No, you can add the spices.
    We have a special onion free sauce.
8. What do you recommend?
    Today's special is fresh fish.
    The chef's specialty is pasta.
    The New York steak is delicious.

9. Is everything alright?
   May we have more water?
   Will you cook this more?
   May we have extra dishes?
10. Can you put this in a doggy bag, please?
    Certainly, I'll bring you a box.
    Would you like two boxes?
    Do you want to take everything?

PHRASES TO RECOGNIZE AND REMEMBER

1. How would you like your steak, well-done, medium or rare?
2. The dressings are: Ranch, Blue-cheese, Thousand-islands and vinegar/oil.
3. Please help yourself to the salad bar.
4. Would you care for any drinks before your meal?
5. The sommelier, wine steward, can give you excellent suggestions.
6. We'll have the House wine.
7. This is the à la carte menu and these are our dinner selections.
8. The dinners include soup or salad, the main course, dessert and coffee or tea.
9. Would you care for an appetizer? Here is the list of our appetizers.
10. I'd like a cup of the soup of the day, a chef's salad with blue cheese dressing.
11. May I have the bill please? It was delicious.

CONVERSATIONS

Memorize the sentences then try to write your own conversation

Conversation 1
Complaining about the food

A: The other day at lunch there was a bug in my salad. It made me sick I couldn't eat.
B: Yuck! How awful. You asked for another salad of course.

5. AT THE RESTAURANT

A: No, I just left it. It's difficult for me to complain or speak up.
B: Oh no! That's the worst thing to do. Complaints and suggestions make things better.
A: Well, I suppose if we are polite in our complaints. It is wrong to ignore mistakes.
B: Exactly! It's crazy not to say something. You still have to pay and tip besides!

Conversation 2
Ordering a meal
A: Are you ready to order? May I take your order?
B: Yes, Thank you. We'll start with the calamari and crispy shrimp appetizers.
A: I'll bring extra sauce for everyone.
B: Then she'll have the New York steak dinner and I'd like the Lobster special.
A: Very good. How would you like the steak? Can I bring you some drinks now?
B: Rare please. Yes, we'll start with a white wine but may I see the wine list, please.

Conversation 3
Write your *Restaurant* conversation using vocabulary words.
A:
B:
A:
B:
A:
B:

FILL IN THE BLANKS

From the list below select the correct word or words to complete the sentences.

water   buzz   appetizers   house specialty   à la carte   wine steward   alcohol dessert   salad bar   medium rare   menu

1. We'll _____ you with this pager when your table is ready.
2. You may order a complete meal or _____, just getting what you want.
3. Our fried rice is the _____ of our chef.
4. We'd like to start with some _____. Can you recommend something?
5. Please bring _____ as well as the other drinks.
6. I'd like my steak _____, please.
7. Help yourself to drinks from that machine and salad at the _____.
8. I'm sorry we don't have a license to serve _____ or beer.
9. The _____ can offer you excellent suggestions for choosing a wine.
10. Soup or salad and coffee and _____ are included with the dinner selections.

ESSAY

Write your *Restaurant* story. Use words and sentences in this chapter.

6. GOING SHOPPING
FINDING THE BEST BUY

SITUATION

You have perhaps limited time and a limited budget for shopping. You are wondering where you can find the best buys for your money. Shopping may be the main purpose of your trip and finding that perfect memento or treasure can be a lot of fun. On the other hand, shopping for a specific item or buying things because they seemed like a bargain can become a nightmare if we don't pay attention. In the United States shopping is almost a national pastime, and the stores open early and close late. Malls with department stores, restaurants, boutiques, brand-name stores and specific item stores have become a shopper's paradise. 'One stop' shopping has everything! Malls cover large areas and you can walk many miles within the Mall. Shopkeepers, salespeople work shifts so the Mall is open every day from early morning until late at night seven days a week. This is all for our shopping convenience.

In Europe, however, it may be very different. Shops are more individual and shopkeepers may take long lunch breaks or close early in the evenings or they may not even be open on the weekends. In special Duty-free shops with your passport and boarding pass, it is possible to buy quality goods cheaper because they are tax free. Also the language is not a problem for you or the salesperson. Meats or plants should only be purchased at the Duty-free areas. They might be confiscated by customs when you return home if the package does not show the proper agriculturally approved seals.

Whether looking for something for yourself, a gift or a special memento, shopping can be fun and challenging. You will enjoy the banter with the salespeople more if before shopping you learn about the currency of the country, sizes of items you might want and some useful phrases. Have fun but be wary of too good of 'a good deal'. Don't be gullible. Know what you want and pay attention. In Japan the customer is king but in other places the saying is: 'Buyer beware'!

WHAT HAPPENS NEXT

1. You have a limited time for shopping but you want to find good bargains.
2. You ask the department salesclerk for the location of the item you are wanting.
3. You have a conversion chart so you know the proper shoe, shirt, and dress size.
4. You have studied the currency exchange rate so you understand the price.
5. You understand some phrases and ask the shopkeeper to give you a better price.
6. You enjoy the bargain banter.
7. You have bought something valuable and you ask for a certificate of authenticity.
8. You buy fresh meats or plants to bring home. You get the official agricultural seal.
9. You ask the shopkeeper if the clothes you have selected need to be dry-cleaned.
10. Your expensive purchase says the 'original duplicate'; you see only the word original!

NEED TO KNOW VOCABULARY

1. Authentic
2. Fitting room
3. Washable
4. Colorfast
5. Wrappings
6. Exchange
7. Receipt
8. Browse
9. Value
10. Guarantee

6. GOING SHOPPING

QUESTIONS AND ANSWERS FOR PAIR TALKING

1. Do you have this in a different material?
   It comes in polyester too.
   We have a different design in 100% cotton.
   This is all we have.
2. Where is the Ladies' department?
   It's on the 2nd floor.
   The entire new store is for Ladies.
   It's the upper 3 floors.
3. What time does the store close?
   We close at 9:30.
   We're open from 10~10.
   We close at 5:30.
4. May I help you?
   No, Thank you I'm just looking.
   No, I'm just browsing.
   Yes, where are the hats?
5. Do you accept traveler's checks?
   Yes, write the date and sign your name.
   Where are you from?
   Write the store name too.
6. Would you like your receipt in the bag?
   Yes, that's fine.
   No, I'll take it.
   May I return this if I don't like it?
7. How are you paying? Are you paying by card?
   Yes, which way do I slide the card?
   Do I press Clear or Enter?
   Do I sign on the machine?
8. When is the clearance sale?
   It starts tomorrow.
   It's happening now.
   Everything must go.
   You'll find great bargains.

9. I have a coupon can you reduce the price?
   I'll give you 20% off.
   That's for another store.
   No, sorry that's expired.
10. There is a one year guarantee do you want the extra 5 year warranty?
    How much more is it?
    What does it include?
    Is there free shipping?

PHRASES TO RECOGNIZE AND REMEMBER
1. Are you in line?
2. Do you want the receipt in the bag?
3. Do you accept yen?
4. May I help you? Just looking, thank you.
5. How does it feel? It's a little big/tight/long/short.

CONVERSATIONS
Memorize the sentences then try to write your own conversation.

Conversation 1
On getting a discount
A: This is nice but it's a little over my budget.
B: I can give you a 10% discount.
A: Oh, that's good but well I'm not sure about the color.
B: It's a very good color for you. Let's see, I'll go as low as 15% off.
A: Really, but to tell the truth I saw this for much less at another store and I just can't decide.
B: All right you beat me. Tell you what, I'll give you a 25% discount but that's my final offer.

6. GOING SHOPPING

Conversation 2
On returning merchandise and complaining
A: I got this here earlier today but I want to return it.
B: Is something wrong? Do you have the receipt?
A: Yes, it's a little bulky. Here is the receipt.
B: Oh. Well we can exchange it for a smaller one or refund your money.
A: Thank you. I really do like it. May I see the smaller one?
B: Certainly. Take your time to decide....I'll be just over there.

Conversation 3
Write your *Shopping* conversation using vocabulary words.
A:
B:
A:
B:
A:
B:

FILL IN THE BLANKS

From the list below select the correct word or words to complete the sentences.

hours   bargain   agricultural seal   washable   browse   receipt   authentic   exchange   Men's department   Duty-free   salesperson

1. I love to shop the _____ tables. You can always get a good buy.
2. Is this _____ or does it need to be dry cleaned?
3. Would you like your _____ or shall I put it in the bag?
4. You realize for that price the watch is a fake. It is not _____.
5. I'd like to _____ this for a smaller size.
6. The store _____ are from 10 AM to 9 PM Monday to Sunday.
7. Where is the _____? I'm looking for dress shirts.
8. I'm just looking, I'd like to _____, thank you.
9. This meat is a gift it has the proper _____ for import.
10. You need your passport to shop at the _____ store.

ESSAY

Write your *Shopping* story. Use the words and sentences in this chapter.

7. GOING SIGHTSEEING
TRAVELING BY BUS, TRAIN OR PLANE DOMESTICALLY

SITUATION

Whether traveling with a tour, with family and friends or by yourself, it is always a good idea to plan ahead. Knowing something about the history, culture and important landmarks of the places you plan to visit will only enhance your trip. Some travelers say they prefer to be surprised with the delights of the trip, the sights and the people. These travelers say that when they return home they prefer to read-up on where they have been and what they have seen. Others say study, be prepared before you go. Know what you are looking at. A little basic knowledge helps build a formative and inquisitive trip. Regardless, if you are seeing natural landscapes, man-made-gardens, viewing historic buildings, cathedrals, temples and other architectural wonders or visiting museums and art galleries, being an informed viewer will double your pleasure. Besides, you may miss a lot if you do not know what you are viewing and you may never have a second chance for the same trip. You are excited about your itinerary.

As well as awareness of what you are seeing, how can you best enjoy the sights? Will you travel by local bus, train or plane? Many places offer discount fares to tourist. Sometimes it is necessary to buy these tickets before you leave home. For example, Japan offers a time limited "rail pass" for visitors from abroad to be purchased in their home country. Taking a package tour means less hassle but also less freedom. You'll find that many landmarks have audio explanations of exhibits, paintings and the wonders for a small fee. Yet as you travel to see all the sights and take all the pictures, remember that is only the first part of your trip. The second part is being able to tell others about the many marvels that you have seen. Keep a diary. Pictures are wonderful but others enjoy your adventures and stories more from the words you use to share your trip. Don't come home with an only, "It was great." Explain how. Give others a descriptive virtual verbal trip. Besides sharing your journey this will give you the opportunity to relive your adventure.

WHAT HAPPENS NEXT

1. You decide to travel abroad with a group of friends. You plan your itinerary.
2. A couple of your friends are excited about the trip but are not interested in preparing.
3. You decide to study about the places and sights you will be seeing.
4. You discover that there are many fascinating places and restaurants and shops.
5. You decide to see as much as possible. This may be your only chance.
6. You inquire about means of local travel, special trains, and bus and plane tickets.
7. You learn that for a small fee you can buy audio explanations of what you see.
8. You take many pictures for yourself and the folks back home.
9. You keep a diary of the funny and quirky things that happen but are easily forgotten.
10. You look forward to sharing your adventure with family and friends when you return.

NEED TO KNOW VOCABULARY

1. Sightseeing tour
2. Package tour
3. Itinerary*
4. Cathedral
5. Museum
6. Architectural wonders
7. Rail Pass
8. Journey
9. Diary
10. Tourist Information Center

7. GOING SIGHTSEEING

QUESTIONS AND ANSWERS FOR PAIR TALKING

1. Where is the best place to see the falls? (Waterfall)
    You can take a boat tour.
    There is a walkway to the top.
    The side view is dynamic.
2. Can you recommend the best time to visit?
    I think just at sunrise is best.
    I think afternoon has the best shadows.
    I think sunset is best.
3. Can we get there by bus?
    Yes, from your hotel.
    A cable car is faster.
    You can walk there in 10 minutes.
4. Is there a connecting flight to the island?
    Yes, everyday at 5.
    Yes, but there is also a boat.
    No, you must return here.
5. What time is the last train?
    The trains operate 24 hours.
    The stations close at 11PM.
    You can always take a taxi.
6. Where is the museum of Natural History?
    All the museums are located in the park.
    It's next to the Art Museum.
    It's in Old Town.
7. Is it possible to walk around the volcano?
    Yes, there is a clear path.
    No, it's too dangerous.
    There is a helicopter tour.
8. I heard there was a secret passage. Can we see it?
    You need a reservation.
    I see you've studied about this place.
    Yes, it's open at 10:00.

9. Do we have time to buy souvenirs?
   Yes, there will be a 30 minute stop.
   Tomorrow is a free day.
   There's a shop in the hotel.
10. May I take pictures?
    No, this area is restricted.
    Yes, of course.
    Shall, I take your picture?

PHRASES TO REMEMBER
1. Where is the best place to view the city?
2. When is a good time to visit?
3. Can you recommend an inexpensive but safe tour?
4. How long will it take?
5. What time is the last train?

CONVERSATIONS
Memorize the sentences then try to write your own.

Conversation 1
A trip within a trip
A: This trip has been so fabulous. I heard we could take a day trip to the mountains.
B: Really, let's do it. Oh, Oh, we didn't bring warn clothes.
A: That's a problem; even in summer the weather changes quickly. We need to be prepared.
B: Maybe we should go to the island instead.
A: Yes, I don't want to waste a moment. Can we get tickets?
B: I saw hydrofoil tickets for sale at the Tourist Bureau. Just the ride will be exciting.

Conversation 2
Getting there... The Best Way
A: It's our first time aboard maybe we should take the package tour?
B: Everything is put together for us and there is free time for local trips.
A: We'll always be with a group. I wonder if we'll have to follow a guide with a flag.
B: Probably. It's a good reliable company so their guides are knowledgeable.
A: Well, we can save our money and go back another time. We might make new friends too.
B: I'm sure it will give us confidence to travel alone next time.

Conversation 3
Write your *Sightseeing* conversation using vocabulary words.
A:
B:
A:
B:
A:
B:

FILL IN THE BLANKS

From the list below select the correct word or word to complete the sentences.

*itinerary   rail pass   souvenirs   package tour   student discounts   view
landmarks   safety feature   sightseeing   local   journal*

1. Be sure to check your _____ for your everyday schedule.
2. This is a _____ so it includes travel, accommodations and some meals.
3. I'd rather shop than go _____.
4. Where can we get a _____ for train travel?
5. Be sure to ask for _____, group tours or senior rates when buying tickets.
6. There is a breathtaking _____ from the top of the tower.
7. When we visit, I want to see all the important _____ of the city.
8. I'm keeping a _____ so that I can share this trip with friends back home.
9. The rails on the path of the waterfall are a _____. It's slippery and dangerous.
10. I hope we have time to buy _____.

ESSAY

Write your *Sightseeing* story. Use the words and sentences in this chapter.

8. MEETING A FAMILY
VISITING A FAMILY OR A HOMESTAY EXPERIENCE

SITUATION

Visiting with a family in a foreign country is a special privilege. Besides the obvious insights into the culture and language, a Homestay experience creates lifelong friendships. Whether you are the guest or the host there are certain rules to follow. First a good host should be concerned about making his homestayer comfortable in his new home. He should not worry about what his home lacks or how the visitor lives in his own country. Rather it is the human touch of kindness, thoughtfulness and sharing that will make the guest feel "at home".

Likewise as a visitor or homestayer, it is important to be receptive to new things. The keyword for the homestayer is *trying*. Expect everything to be different. Expect to help the family and they in turn will help you. For a short time you are a working visitor, learn to expect differences, and accept new responsibilities as an active new family member. Don't think of yourself as a guest to be waited upon, pitch in and help.

Gifts are important when visiting for a long-term stay or just coming for dinner. The gift is a gesture of friendship, not lavish or outlandish. A simple souvenir or sweets are good examples. If you come for dinner you might bring something to drink, the dessert or some flowers. Even as a dinner guest always offer to help: *May I help you with something?* is a polite expression to use.

All is new. Don't be shy. Get out and try to speak. If you are a host, remember your guest will be offering to help but language shy. Give them simple tasks to do. Keep the conversations flowing. Nowadays, there are Homestay opportunities for oldsters as well as youngsters. As the visitor, expect to speak up. Your host may ask you something only once. Say, "Excuse me, once more please." Make your motto: *Speak Help Participate Whatever Whenever Wherever.* A Homestay may be a chance of a lifetime and the beginning of lifelong friendships.

WHAT HAPPENS NEXT

1. You've arranged to stay with a family on your trip abroad.
2. Your family is hosting a foreign visitor.
3. As guest or host good manners are important.
4. As the visitor you expect everything to be different and you expect to *try*.
5. Like in your own family you expect to help and take responsibility.
6. You are invited for a dinner and bring a small gift of wine, flowers or sweets.
7. As a host you remember that your guest is learning the language... you speak clearly.
8. As the visitor you take every opportunity to speak, help and participate.
9. You appreciate that nowadays both young and old can enjoy a Homestay.
10. Your Homestay experience helped you learn the culture now you continue the friendships.

NEED TO KNOW VOCABULARY

1. Foyer / Vestibule / Entrance hall
2. Living room / Dining room
3. Kitchen / Pantry / Washing-Drying / Ironing corner / Mother's Nook
4. Den / Study / Library / Family room / Playroom
5. Bathroom / Toilet / Washroom / Restroom / Ladies room / Bath / Shower
6. Master bedroom / Children's bedroom / Guest room / Spare room
7. Basement / Attic / Garage / Patio / Garden / Porch / Pool

8. MEETING A FAMILY

QUESTIONS AND ANSWERS FOR PAIR TALKING

1. Please make yourself at home. Our home is your home.
    Thank you, it is very kind of you.
    Thank you, please show me what to do.
    Thank you, I'm shy.
2. How may I help you?
    You can set the table, please.
    You can make the children's beds
    You can walk the dog.
3. Where is the vacuum cleaner? Let me vacuum for you.
    Thank you, but it's not necessary.
    That's so kind of you.
    I really appreciate your help.
4. How do I load the dishwasher?
    Put the utensils pointed down.
    All the dishes face the middle.
    Even the pots and pans go in.
5. Where do I take the garbage?
    There's a trash can in the garage.
    Please put the boxes on the curb.
    Separate the bottles.
6. Do you mind if I close my door?
    Of course not.
    You must be tired, please take a nap.
    That's a good idea.
7. How do you remember the words?
    I write everything down.
    I have an electronic dictionary.
    I write new words in a notebook.
8. Do you mind sharing a room?
    Absolutely not, it'll improve my talking.
    I was hoping to share a room.
    That's a good idea.

9. Would you like to go to the movies?
   Great.
   Anytime.
   I hope I can understand something.
   It's a good way to study.
10. Do you want to participate in the activities?
    Yes, I want to do as much as possible.
    It's the fastest way to learn.
    I hope I can.

PHRASES TO REMEMBER

1. It was delicious but I couldn't eat another bite.
2. Thank you but no thank you.
3. Please make yourself at home.
4. How may I help you?
5. Where may I wash up? May I use the bathroom, please?

CONVERSATIONS

Memorize the sentences and try to write your own conversation.

Conversation 1
Participating in family activities

A: Our neighbors have invited us all over for dinner and they want you to come too.
B: Really that's nice but I'm a little timid just now.
A: Don't worry it's a great chance to meet people and the food will be delicious.
B: You're right. Of course I want to go. I just hope I don't make any mistakes
A: Next week there'll be a school dance and then the family's going camping.

B: Wow, you do so much. I really do want to participate. After all, that's why I'm here.

Conversation 2
Doing your share in the family
A: Thank you for keeping your room picked-up. Our children can learn from you.
B: What else can I do to help?
A: Well, there are lots of things that need to be done but walking the dog is a big help.
B: Okay, maybe I can set the table when I get back.
A: Your mother taught you well how to help in a family. Sharing the work gives us all time.
B: I'm afraid I was a bit lazy in my own home but I really like helping out here.

Conversation 3
Write your *Homestay* conversation using vocabulary/text words.
A:
B:
A:
B:
A:
B:

FILL IN THE BLANKS

From the list below select the correct word or words to complete the sentences.

chores   trying   basement   mother's nook   manners   volunteer
living room   pantry   family room   host   house exchange

1. I'm _____ new things on this homestay. Living in a different culture is exciting.
2. My _____ family has already sent me pictures.
3. When in doubt about what to do, good _____ can smooth the way.
4. The _____ is used for guests and entertaining.
5. The _____ is a small closet in the kitchen to store food and household supplies.
6. My house mom has her own _____ in the kitchen for menu planning and study.
7. The _____ is where the family gathers to watch TV and play games.
8. The _____ was like a separate apartment under the house.
9. I want to make my best effort so I'll _____ to help.
10. In a family there are always _____, lots of house job to do.

ESSAY

Write your *Meeting a Family* story. Use words and sentences in this chapter.

9. AT THE THEATER
ENCOUNTERING CULTURE AND ENTERTAINMENT

SITUATION

A night at the theater, opera, or symphony is exciting and calls for dressing up. Before arriving in casual travel attire it is best to call the management and find out what is the appropriate dress. Semi-formal wear means 'dressy' for ladies and 'black tie', suit for men. Tuxedo and gowns are formal 'white tie' but acceptable. If you are comfortable it is not 'over dressing'. Of course there are also matinees or afternoon performances available. Dress is more informal at a matinee.

During Intermission refreshments are served in the lobby as a service or for a small fee. Here the guests mingle and exchange small talk. Before you leave on your trip you might inquire if it is possible to include theater tickets in your itinerary. If all else fails it might be possible to obtain seats the night of the performance on a first-come-first-served basis. Also the balcony seats high in the theater, close to the ceiling, can offer the best choice for acoustics. These are inexpensive tickets but also a distance from the stage. Season tickets are a good idea if you plan on living in the area. All events offer season tickets for a reduced price and you are guaranteed your favorite seat. This is a good cultural investment and a good way to develop language skills.

Going to the movies is much more casual. Besides ordinary cinemas, there are also outdoor theaters and Drive-in-theaters. Here it is possible to watch a movie from your car. Some people go to the movies to relax or even sleep. Others enjoy the fast food and junk snacks, ice-cream, buttered popcorn, candies, or soft drinks. Alcoholic drinks are usually not sold. When buying your ticket inquire if there are discounts, for example: student, group or senior golden fares.

Outdoor concerts or sporting events are even more casual. Sometimes they include a picnic or a barbeque. This means you must bring your own refreshments, food and drink. If you are invited to such an event be sure to ask what you should bring. Come prepared for the cold night air even in the summer heat. Some events may last many hours.

When visiting a foreign country it is exciting to take in the cultural events such as opera, ballet, theater, symphony, concerts, cinema and sports. You might even be surprised by Karaoke. Don't worry about the language. It is the ambiance that you will enjoy. Have a good time.

WHAT HAPPENS NEXT

1. You've purchased an opera ticket and are wondering what the appropriate dress is.
2. You are excited about attending this grand cultural event. You consider the matinee.
3. You are excited about the Intermission time and the chance to mingle with other guests.
4. There were still tickets available for the concert on a first-come-first-served basis.
5. If you move to the area you will definitely buy season tickets for events.
6. With season tickets you have good seating.
7. You enjoy going to the movies and seeing films without subtitles.
8. You are becoming a fan of movie junk food....oh..no.
9. You notice the many opportunities for music in the park and other outdoor events.
10. Attending these cultural events has been a highlight of your trip.

NEED TO KNOW VOCABULARY

1. Intermission
2. Small talk / Refreshments
3. Matinee
4. First-come-first-served
5. Fast food / junk food / Barbeque / B-B-Q
6. Reserved Seats
7. Broadway Play
8. Off Broadway

9. AT THE THEATER

9. Live Concert
10. Symphony

QUESTIONS AND ANSWERS FOR PAIR TALKING

1. Have you gotten your tickets yet?
   I have tickets for the opera.
   I have tickets for the symphony.
   I have tickets for the matinee.
2. Do you have appropriate dress?
   I packed a suit for the occasion.
   I'll buy something there.
   My friend will lend me something.
3. What do you talk about during Intermission?
   It's a chance to meet people.
   You can talk about the event.
   The weather is a good topic.
4. What kinds of refreshments are served at the opera, symphony or theater?
   Bite size snacks are popular.
   Wine or champagne is sold.
   Small sweets are available.
5. Have you seen any movies yet?
   I'm hoping to see an adventure film.
   I've only seen the TV movies.
   I saw a hit show.
6. Do you buy junk snacks at the movies?
   Of course, that's why I go.
   I like the jumbo drinks.
   I don't like eating in theaters.
7. Can we get tickets for the game?
   We should be able to buy at the gate.
   We can get them from the hotel.
   Tonight is sold out.

8. The concert is in the park what are you bringing?
   I'll bring a blanket and coat.
   I'll bring some drinks and snacks.
   I'll bring bread and cheese.
9. What does BYO for BBQ mean?
   It means 'Bring your own for the barbeque'.
   Bring your own food.
   It's whatever you want.
10. Did you understand any of the dialogue at the play?
    I enjoyed the ambiance.
    I got the general idea.
    It was well worth the trip.

PHRASES TO REMEMBER

1. Advanced reservations
2. Black Tie required
3. Who is the composer/soloists/conductor/director/playwright/actor?
4. What's playing?
5. Who's in it?

CONVERSATIONS

Memorize the sentences then try to write your own conversation.

Conversation 1
Dressing up

A: Is there a difference between White Tie and Black Tie for a theater or dinner invitation?
B: Yes, White Tie means a Tux for men and a long evening gown for ladies.
A: Oh, I see. It's a dress code. So, White Tie means very formal.
B: Exactly, Black Tie is semi-formal; men can wear suit/jacket, ladies cocktail dress.

9. AT THE THEATER

A: Now I'm confused. What does that mean?
B: Women have more freedom in their fashion but usually it means a knee length dress.

Conversations 2
At the Baseball game
A: We have behind home plate seats for the game tonight. They're best in the house.
B: You play baseball in a house, here?
A: No, that's just an expression. I hope we can see some terrific hits.
B: Maybe we'll even catch a pop-up foul ball.
A: Well, we'd better go if we're going to get to the game in time for the "Star Spangled Banner".
B: I'm so excited. Hot dogs and cracker jacks, singing the baseball song too! Hurry let's go!

Conversation 3
Write your *Theater / Events* conversation using vocabulary words.
A:
B:
A:
B:
A:
B:

FILL IN THE BLANKS

From the list below select the correct word or words to complete the sentences.

matinee   appropriate   reserved seats   black tie   what's playing   dialogue acoustics   stadium   performances   intermission   fast food

1. I'm so excited we have _____ for the opera tonight.
2. I heard the dress code was _____.
3. The higher up you go in the theatre the better the _____, sound, gets.
4. I hope I can understand the _____ of the play.
5. I'm so excited about the small talk and champagne during the _____.
6. We have tickets for the afternoon _____ of this Broadway play.
7. I'll always remember the amazing _____ of the actors and actresses.
8. What is _____ dress for the ballpark this evening?
9. You can buy hot dogs and other _____ at the game.
10. The city uses this _____ for football and baseball games.

ESSAY

Write your *At the Theater story*. Use the words and sentences in the chapter.

10. AT THE SUPERMARKET / DRUGSTORE
GETTING THE THINGS YOU NEED BY YOURSELF

SITUATION

Getting the things you need on your trip by yourself is a great way to boost your confidence. Food shopping can be an adventure and fun. If you've opted to stay in a condominium instead of a hotel, then you may want to try cooking a meal instead of eating out all the time. Visiting the local supermarket, Farmer's Market or even the Mom-Pop stores for supplies will be an eye-opening experience and stimulate your appetite. You might even try self-check-out.

Supermarkets are a great convenience because you can find almost anything you need, with fresh produce, fish, meat, poultry, dairy products, breads and household goods. Many stores include a Delicatessen, with ready-made meals, a bakery, a pharmacy for medicine and a florist. At the meat counter you can ask the butcher for a special cut of meat or the fish-man for his latest catch.

The Deli features ready-made soups or salads, pickles, cheese, various cooked meats, roast-beef or chicken and finger eating snacks. They can also make sandwiches while you wait. They may have a number service system so pay attention to how other customers are served.

The pharmacist is allowed to give advice on symptoms and medication. He is not a doctor but can help you make a good decision. Of course if you take medicine regularly it is best to bring your own from home. If you have jet lag, a cold or upset stomach he can offer advice for the ailment or recommend medication. He can also fill prescriptions if you have gone to a local doctor.

Besides supermarkets many areas offer local produce at Farmer's Markets once a week. Even if you don't purchase anything it is fun to view the local products. Open-air fairs and festivals might also be happening while you travel. These offer a chance to see art and crafts plus new products that may be sold at stores. Some of these things represent the local artist some are traveling booths. You might find something that you fancy but beware of what you are getting. If something or the price is "too good to believe" it usually is flawed or a fake. Keep your eyes and ears open for what is happening in the area. Have fun shopping and looking.

WHAT HAPPENS NEXT

1. You visit the local supermarket to buy or maybe just to get a feeling of the area.
2. You are surprised because the store product arrangement is very similar to home.
3. You try the self-check-out by scanning your purchase just like a clerk. It's very fast.
4. Besides supermarkets there are several small family stores.
5. You like the Delicatessen and find it's an easy place to get a quick sandwich.
6. The bakery and Deli have a box for customers to get a number for service.
7. The pharmacist helps you find some cough medicine.
8. He gives you information about the different choices of medicine.
9. You visit the Farmer's Market and are intrigued by all the outdoor activities
10. You buy a painting of local scenery. You like it so you don't mind the expensive price.

NEED TO KNOW VOCABULARY

1. Eating out / Going to a restaurant
2. Farmer's Market
3. Expiration date
4. Pharmacist / Druggist Pharmacy / Drug Store
5. Prescription
6. Arts and Crafts / Traveling Booths

10. AT THE SUPERMARKET / DRUGSTORE

QUESTIONS AND ANSWERS FOR PAIR TALKING

1. Are you in the express lane?
   No, I have more than 8 items.
   I think so.
   Yes, I have only 5 things.
2. How do I use the self service check-out counter?
   Scan your purchase and deposit the cash.
   Sometimes it doesn't take.
   This is so convenient
3. Do you have soy sauce?
   Yes, Asian foods on aisle 3.
   Yes, on the back wall in the middle.
   Yes, right here.
4. Can I get that with extra rice at the Deli?
   Rice and soup are free.
   We have it with vegetables too.
   Please pack it in 2 boxes.
5. How do you want this meat cut?
   Please slice it as thin as possible.
   In chunks please.
   Like that is okay.
6. What is the catch of the day?
   We have ahi a kind of marlin.
   We have halibut and sole.
   There is no salmon.
7. I have an upset stomach, can you recommend some medicine?
   This is good and has no side effects.
   Yes, any other symptoms?
   Any of these are good.
8. Do you have any allergies or special problems when taking medicine?
   No, nothing.
   I'm allergic to clams and shrimp.
   I have hay fever.

57

9. Are you eating? How is your appetite?
   It's okay, I'm eating fine.
   I feel sluggish and tired.
   I'm not very hungry.
10. Have you been to the street festival yet?
    I hear there's music.
    Artist and craftsmen display their work.
    There's so much local color.

PHRASES TO RECOGNIZE AND REMEMBER
1. This is the express lane. (8-10 items limit)
2. Check the expiration date.
3. Are you taking any other medication?
4. How is your appetite?
5. Consult your doctor when you get home.

CONVERSATIONS
Memorize the sentences then try to write your own conversation.

Conversation 1
At the Supermarket

A: There is such a wide selection of fresh foods and cooked foods. What should we get?
B: Well at the Deli they have meals and we can cook and refrigerate things in our room.
A: Okay, let's get something easy at the Deli now, and then try to cook in the condominium.
B: That sounds perfect. I'm hungry, but I want to try some of this fresh fish and fruit.
A: They sell small bags of rice too. Wow, we can save a lot by cooking ourselves.

10. AT THE SUPERMARKET / DRUGSTORE

B: Of course eating out is fun too, but we can go out later and see the town.

Conversation 2
Talking to the Pharmacist
A: I have a bad sunburn can you recommend something please.
B: Of course, do you have any allergies?
A: No, I have never had any problems.
B: Okay, have you been vaccinated for tetanus?
A: Yes, I had all my shots. What does that have to do with sunburn?
B: Nothing. I was just curious about things in your country. This lotion will relieve the pain.

Conversation 3
Write your *Supermarket / Pharmacy* conversation using vocabulary words.
A:
B:
A:
B:
A:
B:

FILL IN THE BLANKS

From the list below select the correct word or words to complete each sentence.

Farmer's Market   express lane   appetite   variety   prescription   aisles expiration date   eye-opening   sluggish   thinly slice   check-out

1. You have only 7 items so please use the _____.
2. The supermarket has a _____ of inexpensive fruits and vegetables.
3. The _____ is open every Friday from 10 AM to 2 PM on 4th street.
4. Before you buy milk or eggs be sure to check the _____.
5. I like the wide _____ in the supermarket. It's so easy to shop.
6. I want to make sukiyaki, can you _____ this beef, please.
7. I brought my doctor's _____ from Tokyo. I hope you can refill it.
8. I think I must be getting a cold. I'm not hungry. I don't have an _____.
9. I feel a bit _____ maybe I have jet-lag and just need more sleep.
10. Excuse me, are you in line for _____?

ESSAY

Write your *Supermarket / Pharmacy* story. Use the words and sentences in the chapter.

Notes

【著者紹介】

Robin J. OKANO （ロビン・J・オカノ）

米国カリフォルニア州バークレイに生まれる。

1964年　NHK教育テレビ 英会話講師
1966年　上智大学卒業
1968年　米国 ミシガン大学大学院 日本研究科修士課程修了
1970年　国際青年交流委員会において英語による日本史・アメリカ史の講師
1977年　流通経済大学 経済学部講師
現　在　同大学 社会学部教授

THE LITTLE BOOK OF TRAVEL

発行日　2012年2月25日　初版発行
　　　　2015年4月1日　第二刷発行
著　者　Robin J. OKANO
発行者　佐伯 弘治
発行所　流通経済大学出版会
　　　　〒301-8555　茨城県龍ヶ崎市120
　　　　電話 0297-64-0001　FAX 0297-64-0011

ⒸR. J. OKANO　　　　　　　　Printed in Japan/アベル社
ISBN 978-4-947553-55-3 C2082 ¥600E